Garden of the
Midnight Rosary

For my special love
Kittisaro

Bridge Verse

Said Jesus, on whom be peace,
'This world is but a bridge,
pass over it.
Do not build your house there.
Those who hope for an hour
may hope for eternity.
The world is but a bridge,
spend it in devotion.
The rest is unseen.'

Found on a bridge in Northern India

Garden of the Midnight Rosary

Poems by Thanissara

SACRED MOUNTAIN PRESS

Published by   Sacred Mountain Press
              Dharmagiri
              P. O. Box 270
              Underberg 3257
              KwaZulu-Natal, South Africa
              E-mail: dragonmtn@xsinet.co.za

ISBN 0 620 28726 8 (Hardcover)
ISBN 0 620 28558 3 (Softcover)

Cover design by Anthony Cuerden
Design and typesetting by Sally Hines

Printed and bound by Interpak Books, Pietermaritzburg

Contents

Part Five CELEBRATION

Acknowledgments

My profound appreciation and gratitude to Mr Gordon Fox for encouraging this collection of poems from start to finish. Without his gentle and thoughtful support throughout the last ten years, it would not have seen the light of day.

Immense gratitude to the Libra Foundation for expressing faith in humanity through its many compassionate projects and for sponsorship of this book.

To the University of California Press for the permission to re-print the closing homage taken from the beautiful rendering of the *Ramayana* by William Buck.

To Kittisaro for patient help with editing.

To Doriaan Harhoff for invaluable suggestions.

To Sally Hines for taking it over the last hurdle.

To Anthony Cuerden for the cover design.

Free Will Offering

This book is to be given out on a Dana (free will offering) basis. Any donations offered in response will support Dharmagiri Buddhist Hermitage and its Outreach programmes which presently support rural education and care in response to the HIV/AIDS crisis in KwaZulu-Natal, South Africa. For further information contact:

Dharmagiri
P. O. Box 270
Underberg 3257
KwaZulu-Natal, South Africa
E-mail: dragonmtn@xsinet.co.za

Foreword

I have been much inspired by the gentle and generous ways of meditation that Mary Thanissara Peacock teaches. Her simple and profound way of explaining the intricacies of Buddhist practices has helped me, my wife June, many of my friends and others who have spent some time with Thanissara at her retreats. But, when I receive unexpectedly, a collection of poetry, I was pleasantly surprised to know that Thanissara is also a poet of similar simplicity and profoundness. Reading her poems I experienced the same stillness, the same silence and the same serenity as in meditation. I found the poems to be meditations on the moments of hidden beauty, unfolding like the lotus petals with the rise of the morning sun.

The poems are as much mystical as romantic. Thanissara's voice reminds me of the songs of Meera, the Indian mystic poet and lover of Krishna and the poems of Wordsworth rolled into one. Hildergard of Bingen in the Christian tradition and Jelaluddin Rumi in the Sufi tradition have celebrated that marriage of romantic and mystic spirit. But, in the Buddhist tradition, such poetry is rare. In *The Garden of the Midnight Rosary*, Thanissara fills that space.

In her poems, the rivers of passion and compassion confluence. In her imagination, 'death is just the wedding night' and we are all the 'dreamers of an eternity'. Thanissara builds the bridges of longing which take her to the field of belonging.

> That your grace should come unbidden
> streaming through me.
> What is it that makes me want to know you
> when you slip through my constant grasp.
> The sweetness of this longing
> raises church spires
> ecstatic choirs and lonely fasting.

Without longing there is non-belonging. But, most of our longing and belonging roams at a superficial and mundane level. We are caught in craving and grasping trivial and banal desires. Thanissara's poems take us beyond the slipping worlds, beyond wounded desires, into the level where we are on the other shore and there the meeting of love is so graceful that the physical and celestial merge where the invisible faces are in intimate embrace.

I hope that others will find these poems as moving, as mysterious and as inspiring as I have found them.

Satish Kumar
Hartland, Devon, England
October 2001

Introduction

Mary Thanissara Peacock has given us a cycle of poetry so imbued with profound insight, beauty beyond words, and 'medicinal support' for what it is to be human that the most honorable words I can offer at the outset are to advise the reader to skip ahead and begin reading the poetry now. You will indeed be taken on a journey, *As the great wheel of time/ rolls silent/ through our intimate heart,/ like beads of a rosary/ round and round.* You will engage in an illuminating walk of the labyrinth: inward and outward to inward again, backwards in time and forwards, around the circle, until, surrounded by *The Garden of the Midnight Rosary*, you are left to rest in timeless stillness and peace.

Poetry can be the gold at the end of a mysterious alchemical process. It satisfies our need for structure and logic, for rhythm and continuous music; it can tell an epic story and fill our minds with cinematic images; it reaches into the deepest dreaming part of ourselves with healing power. *The Garden of the Midnight Rosary* brings us vivid color and sound, emotional impact, a flow of visions. Thanissara's poetry puts us in touch with the cosmic dimension of reality, makes us well again as we read.

The inner journey of this poetry is informed by Thanissara's years of meditation practice and contemplation, her marriage to Kittisaro, her travels, and her close affinity to other cultures and times. Thanissara's openness – to life, to art, to the world's religions with their rich and varied iconography, and to history deeply felt – has given her the literary sensibilities to express her highly developed spiritual awareness. The influence of great poets of both English and Irish literature and of the East is evident in her range of shapes, tones and rhythms. There is a strong feminine voice in her exploration of being alive, proceeding through the personal experiences of longing, love, loneliness, inevitable loss, to the vast human questions of the horror of war and the force of ignorance. She begins with transcendence and meaning, *This attraction to another/ in the kernel of the universe/ where all life starts.*

The universal themes explored in the five parts are passionate, deeply felt, joyous and ultimately profoundly peaceful. Each poem is a prayer, and so is the collection as a whole. Just as the earth turns upon its own axis in a rotating solar system in a spinning galaxy, so does each poem – each bead of the rosary – turn, complete in itself, containing all the elements of the whole. The image in 'Circles' shows the beads in motion, *Turning through a curve/ of peaceful spinning,/ within an orbit/ led by an intimate song.* And the whole rosary turns, a mandala of sometimes terrifying beauty. In Thanissara's garden, there are many encounters with paradox – of night and day, light and dark, death and life, earth and water, war and peace, personal love and loss – which weave human experiences into a cosmic perspective. There are turnings within turnings, and all a prayer.

The first part of the book, 'Journey', introduces stunning images of the natural world that are prominent throughout the cycle. Magnificent birds appear, alive with totemic energy: raven, swan, skylark, geese. An *egret/ stands patient in moonlit water.* Later, *the sacred ibis spreads her wings/ in devotion to the way/ drops of nectar swirl/ through every atom, particle and cell.* Where most needed, among the many wondrous birds there appears a phoenix. In 'Sunbird' the poet herself is a bird. Flowers are stunningly instructive, and we may be reminded of the monk Kassapa, who immediately grasped the truth of aliveness in the moment when he saw the Buddha gaze on a single flower. We are after all in a Garden, a garden which contains all the joys and all the sorrows of human experience.

The second part, 'Wilderness', begins with an invitation to *take a walk,/ into the wilderness/ at the quiet time of day.* The wilderness is 'bleeding' here. *Desert thorns pierce the skin of our longing.* We forget *from where we come/ and to where we go.* Yet there is reassurance. *For out of the cooled ashes,/ will come a new way.* This reassurance grounds the poet, and us readers, in compassion and wisdom sufficient to withstand a profound look into our personal mortality and into the great grief of what we humans are doing to one another and to this sacred planet. We are guided through images of ignorance, of the devastation of technology, and of nuclear holocaust. *Towers of dead trees/ turn worlds of words/ into spinning, numb, weeping sounds.*

The poem 'Eternal Knots' strikes a chillingly appropriate note in these militant times. *Inside high walls/ minds sealed in cold steel/ seasoned by aversion/ masked as fairness./ Righteousness holds sway/ as iron birds, wings tipped in terror,/ cast shadows over diminishing landscapes./ Burnt and tortured earth.* Later we read *The clawed beast lumbers through scorched ground, an ice crazed demon from hell, eating corpses from vast wars.* The line, *Pieces float in my mind,* suggests the Bodhisatva Avalokiteshvara. The suffering of this world shatters his mind into pieces. The poet takes us through a similar process towards a way to live in this world, as it is. *In the wounded wasteland/ where the fiery crucible dries incessant waves/ of sorrow and desire,/ we sit and sweat away our impurity in the fire.*

In the third part, 'Opening', we are led out of the wilderness, into our hearts *waterfall of graceful belonging* and into some of the great religious traditions. Shiva speaks. *This universe turns/ just for the love of it.* Vajra Guru and *Primordial mind like the sky* appear, the Buddha, and the ever present inspirational power of the earth.

'Return', features images of the Sacred Feminine. We are treated to the Lady of Avalon, Kali, the Black Madonna and Kuan Yin. In 'Mother of the Buddha' the great strengths of both the masculine and feminine traditions are juxtaposed. The feminine, thus acknowledged, is a crucial key to the healing of deeper splits in our culture and civilisation, *rhythms dance/ a melting vigilance.*

'Celebration', the final part, closes with the jewel-like 'Fire Minder'. The fire minder tends the light, which can only manifest in the darkness. Those dark time-spaces in the rosary garden, as we have seen, are shot through with peace, awareness of love, natural connection with the earth, appreciation of the stark beauty of life, and ecstatic states. All sorrows and joys are cradled in Thanissara's garden of poetry. Living in our dear animal bodies, with our complicated pulsing minds, it's a stretch for most of us to look deeply at our own mortality, and the poet's guidance is precious. True to her insights in Buddhist meditation practice, her words help us to open to and embrace even our own personal death, and beyond that, to find ourselves in the turnings, small and large, which mark our deepest human experiences.

Cathy Wickham,
San Francisco
California
Janurary 2002

**To Sri Hanuman
Protector of Poets**

Sri Hanuman,
Son of the Wind
breath of Ram
friend of friends,
breathe your ocean of grace.

Sri Ram
as a thousand suns,
blissful luminous and divine
is your exquisite gaze.
This entire world
unfolds at your feet
as just your cheerful play.

Lord of the Universe
every being is your servant.
Within your vast spheres
those free of ego offer all glories to you.
Our existence is constantly remade
after your sight has burnt us through.
Our wholeness is laid open
when in service of you.

We praise your light.
We praise your power.
We praise your many names
like stars that wheel night and day.

Sri Hanuman.
Protector of Poets,
friend of those who love the Dharma.
Take us in your breath
to the other shore.
Take us
so we may be released
from all attachments.

This ocean so vast and long,
our strength fails
and heart falters
without your grace
to carry us over.

Dear Hanuman, Friend Hanuman,
Bhajelo Ji Hanuman.

Sri Ram
Sri Hanuman
Sri Sri Sri Neem Karoli Baba Santa Maharaj

Journey

Day Prayer

This prayer I have,
silent and formless,
rolls across untold landscapes
painted with each moment's detail.
This prayer,
like the beating of soft wings
against a night lamp,
threads my days.
It is like dawn dew
waiting to evaporate
or a ragged child
walking the market place.

My prayer is like
petals opening to the sun.
Or the way an egret
stands patient in moonlit water
its neck gently curved,
while the sun
already set
leaves sweeps
of gold and red,
enfolding me
in the silence
that everywhere
sings the prayer
that long ago
you gave me.

Arriving

The lost ark
in ancient fields and oceans wide
rippling in waters rising
the tides of our arriving.
Go wherever you will
in those familiar moments
and see your face again.

That your grace should come unbidden
streaming through me . . .
What is it that makes me want to know you
when you slip through my constant grasp.
The sweetness of this longing
raises church spires
ecstatic choirs and lonely fasting.
Through the pages of our journey
at the edge of different seas
when death is just the wedding night.
At the shrine of our forgetting
in the many lands of your dominion,
for you, I'll light a candle there.

In the flickering flame of my passing
your unformed breath
moves through
the cells of my belonging
and carries me to the shore.

Night Boat

In the time of crossing
silent pages of my journey
fall onto forgotten land.

You hold my hand
within tides of destiny
that are shaped
in half sight
dimmed by the fever
of our careless wanting.
That half formed feeling,
the habitual instinct
coursing deep beneath us
in a river of passion
sweeping to its consummation.

In the waters of aloneness
drifting . . .

On my night boat
bathed in
moonlight casting
over a green sea.
A reminder
of what is inscribed
in the folds of our story,
that one day
at the end of all wanting,
like sunlight racing across water,
you will come for me.

Searching

This is how long I've searched
the mystery of our vow,
throwing pennies in the wishing well
held in your unseen breath
moving us so close together
through the veils
I daily bow.

For you I've travelled down
this lonely road of the anointed,
releasing
borrowed defences as I go,
bowing
to dry bones and fire.

The hushed wind carries my prayer
through stained glass
to empty rooms.
When least expected
your brief arrival
tempts with dream whispers.
I know your presence
through the heart pain pulsing
like a lover, there and gone.
I see your pastel brush across the sky
and I know the illusion of my longing
before your equal eye.

What will you offer
as I travel the thirst of my desire?
Listen, I'll lay down my wanting
and wait again for you
in the ashes of this pyre.

Home

I like to stroll
in the cool evening
along the water's edge
among wild lilies.
I'd also like to find a way home
through the many lives I roam.
We are dreamers of an eternity
when we only have this moment
in which to be.
Across this lone journey
I live the dwindling days
as my own heart's refugee.

In India at the tea stall
I wept when a twelve-year-old boy
in his holed T-shirt
cleaning unkind tables
was more at home than me.
Even great symphonies
in the notes that fall from heaven
are more at home
than their composers could ever be.

Some people never look to the stars
and they mistake the singing noises
and graceful leaning to express our exile
as dangerous movements of the mad.

Only take a stroll where the water laps at your feet,
where all the glories of an empire
do not soothe the soul
as one perfect lily
swaying in the breeze.

The Bell

I follow with slow steps
the footprints you leave
and the insistent sound
you weave in the circle
of our separation.
Across the river wide
where the sacred ibis
spreads her wings
in devotion to the way,
drops of nectar swirl
through every atom,
particle and cell.

The candle burns so low in the latticed castles
where a faint glow down dark hallways
shines behind the door of your promise.
The songs of all time reach into
the crown of my belonging
as I breathe
the faint trace of your arrival,
exploding and imploding
the pieces of my life.

Through cascading notes
and distant times
as you ring the bell,
I hear once more
your singing sound excel.

Violet Flower

Craving is deep in these bones.
Death is on the highway
stalking, moving, breathing in gasps.
The rain pours down
on those soaked, blessed
in floods swept
to a surging river
of cleansed torn bodies
and dreams unspoken,
quietly gone
to the next world.
Yet the sun will arrive again
for those still standing.

Heart unfolding, holy fire in these bones,
blessed breath moving flesh
in the night alone.
Sparks of fire blowing in the wind
to ignite and devastate
in that same countryside
with grass, heather, dandelion and delicate buds.

What beauty, what splendour,
going on and on to
'This is the Voice of America calling',
spinning realities that imprison
time, meaning and importance.

Take it seriously
or take it lying down
in a garden at twilight,
while wood smoke drifts,
looking up at an evening star.

Let importance die away
and the need for power soften.
Expect nothing and see
your own heart's strength
stay constant through eternity.

Like a cork on the ocean
the mind floats free,
the breath flows in and out completely.
And so
the fire going cool,
the river with bodies, froth and tree
flowing to the sea,
curling into a field of memory
entwining us together,
bridging many dawns
and curving into tomorrow.

See the violet flower.
How perfectly it blooms.

Circles

See your life as a circle
somehow
come round again.
You visited here already,
but now arrive with different eyes
restored from before,
the grave long dug,
sung hymns faded and organ notes gone.
A forgotten past
covered by white lilies of the valley
perpetually flowering over the seasons,
turning through a curve
of peaceful spinning
inside an unknown orbit,
led by an intimate song.
The notes we dream
invite a fall to the centre
where we wonder how to be
in such a vastness
stretching away to infinity.

Endless still turning,
leaf, city and sea,
trekking the blackest space,
a gentle rotating earth
radiating bright
from sun and star light.
While we in our daily minutiae
. . . bewildered . . .
in a swirling sea of change
which crashes

without asking nicely,
like . . . let's take tea and talk calmly
about this familiar impersonality
washing all away.

We are washed away
into tomorrow's sand
dissolved into cells
snaking within a cosmos
turning round and round
over the land,
in cycles
of perfect
karmic destiny.

Flowers At Your Feet

Over the bridge of my longing
where I burn through the legacy of desire,
far from the lonely sculptors,
is the place we meet
to leave this world behind.

There, pink climbing roses
trail the forbidden room
where I enter my losses
so I don't remember
that ever there was the pain,
the in-turned heat
of my helpless falling away from you.

The river flows beneath us
and the night folds around
another time –
when the garden gate opened so freely.

In the dreams of our meeting
through the apple orchard
near the still lake,
white swans gather in
brilliant colours across the sky.

So graceful,
the lines of your body,
the flowers at your feet.
The intimate embrace
that allows a glimpse
of your invisible face.

Midnight Rosary

Midnight hint
of silent sound
with beads clicking.
Light blue candle
burning slowly
blending sandalwood scent
in haze smoke
mingled with entreaty.
Prayers lift
gently
into ether
caressing and
mixing
into the
many reflections
of our one face.

Wilderness

The Quiet Time of Day

Let us walk into the wilderness
at the quiet time of day.
In the glow of the setting sun
red sparkles shower upon our heads
and birds fly happily on their way.

Let's go even further
beyond the circle of these minds
busy thinking the matrix of time
like a towering edifice that casts
its uncertain phantom canopy
on the pristine clarity of here and now,
as we walk from past identity.

Desert thorns pierce the skin of longing
and quiet tears fall for all that is gone
to the halls of distant memory.
All which is never to arrive again
haunts the hushed moments
where within strange dreams
we pass each other by.

The searching days that echo
the phoenix's timeless song
undulating over dale and valley
carried by bird and sea
through our time laden reverie.
The bleeding wilderness
where an aged dark shadow
falls across our soul
so we forget from where we come
and to where we go.

Let us take a walk at the quiet time of day.
Faith calls and as night falls
the sky's primordial adornments
trace a destined future
of uncertain tomorrows.
This day,
the song so lyrical
unfolding so gradual,
the seed already coded,
planted, flowering and dissipated,
the times to come, already visited.

The steps of belief
taken over a disintegrating road
passing under a night bridge.
The icon within my heart, already eclipsed.
The unsure companion found at every road bend,
faith between doubt,
life between deaths,
coming and going that leaves no tracks.

Let us walk the naked desert.
Poets will soothe, love will inspire,
the earth will fill our desire.
Holy ash adorns the way
and a full moon will rise to anoint
this transformation through fire.

Gently, bone prayer beads – om mani –
caressed – padme hum –
in the wilderness – om mani –
at the quiet time of day – padme hum –
for out of cooled ashes – om –
in the pause between – mani –
comes a new way – padme hum.

Courage

There is something ancient that obstructs
my heart's desire to know its fullness.
Instead in the fading light
I slip into my wound
to let night dreams heal what they can,
so that once again I can find the courage
to merge with each breath
when meeting this new day.

We Are Captive Here

We are captive here
in dust, in city, in the hours that tick by,
a butterfly wrapped in a cocoon,
a seed waiting to bloom.
In a café on the windy dock side,
shadows echo a trapped isolation
meshed in soiled walls
where tea waits to cool.
While an old song plays again and again
ships head out to sea.

Seagulls fly high
over tramps on a park bench.
On Chelsea bridge lamps shine bright.
In that same stone church
a deserted priest robed in purple
drones tired lessons of morality.
With snow on the ground,
it's a cold and bitter night.

Ave Maria,
the Tigris and Euphrates,
your tears flow to the great seas
and coil through cities
that weep unearthly sounds
sealed within tides of our denial.
The hollowness that moves fervent rounds
of amber threaded beads
worn through ceaseless creeds.
Return to the grave today,
the long night wakes early to pray.

In every moment a finality,
an unknown answer
inviting a timeless reach
where ships drift without destination,
passing memories along the lines of time.

Enter death's quiet gate
and float in a great sea
through tides of incarnation
to arrive at a new harbour,
really a circle to a familiar before.

Here, walking the endless labyrinth,
separate from the sure,
in the midst of all that's changing
we feel the silent urge reciting,
'just once more'.

To tread these same streets again
with different feet but same intent.
To celebrate the star filled sky,
the clouds, the moon and dragonfly.

Though it takes many a tomorrow
to weave into that end
perpetually longed for . . .
on a ship floating far
from the receding shore.

Nuclear Times

Lining the great avenue,
trees and breathing things
comfort each other
in the house of darkness
with shards of light
fading –
And I dream
of times when blazing presence
consumed illusion's might.

Far below,
in the constant stream
where each day we breathed full
earthy smells and dripping juices
of nectar and ripe insights.
Where silence was comfortable
and spoke of ancient rhythms
in the halls eternal.

Now,
House of Shadows,
the oceans rush in,
collapsing empires
and hopeful dreams
come tumbling down.
Fused fire and atom
explodes apart.
Nuclear fission
blows out naïve longing
as weeping sounds,
wailing and gnashing,
spiral in derelict rounds.

The slouching beast has arrived
into the house of screens.
Night dreams
filled with children's screams
as we run –
from the wave of past holdings
hurtling us together
in a fiery roll
of cement, uranium,
flesh and bones,
memories and picture frames –
to oblivion.

The hollow land moans,
the breast fast withers
and the light,
now eclipsed,
crosses to shadows.

Beyond Control

It is beyond our control.
We are walking
into forces beyond our control,
into a burning axis of denial
as this weary planet shudders
in the soundless night.

There's something inside pushing,
some ancient urge eating us through.
We are the driven ones
drinking dry the breast,
riding the thawing warm hide,
pushing deeper into the slippery well.
There is no return.

Prophets see the future times
shaped by poisonous desire
of corporate thirst
seething through virgin lands
where dry winds blow.
Hot and scorched rain falls
as wild tigers roar their dying call.

Unchecked will hardened in iron flesh
striding across laced webs of intricacy,
grown these million years.
Genetic codes and cyber chips
cradled in shallow hands
devouring the future's birthright
as we sink in the quicksands
of rampant appetite gorging
on a daily spillage of news.

Towers of dead trees
turn worlds of words
into spinning, numb,
weeping sounds
as the earth haunts,
with a melancholy lament,
the wilderness of our wasted hearts.

In different frequencies whales sing
and oceanic tides flow
into our desolate souls
as we sink in cold fury.
In night dreams we sweat
and move in the mystery.

See how a small yellow flower
pushes through concrete
to open delicate petals to the dawn.
Why are we not in awe?

We are frozen
in narrow armour,
hidden under a glittering cloak.
Feel it in the frustration
as we sit apart from one another
in cosy armchairs,
our roots withered,
lost in time,
dissolved in space.

Across the far oceans
a lone bagpipe
mourns
our silent tears.

Slipping Worlds

A house of different faces
looking in
while sensations flow
through my body in waves
as I
stand
down
into the ground.
Down where I feel
the universe spinning
and the lines slipping.

Momentarily,
leaves catch sun
as I expand to meet
the waves that move inward
at the speed of thought.
Recitations round the rosary
collapse my world
into decreasing circles
as I reach out to taste tears,
to catch a smile.

While slipping to
being already here.
I am already dead,
trying to awaken
in a house of faces
dissolving to a centre,
looking out.

Eternal Knots

1.
Inside high walls, minds sealed in cold steel
seasoned by aversion masked as fairness.
Righteousness holds sway,
icy aloofness drains the light away
as iron birds, wings tipped in terror,
cast shadows over diminishing landscapes.
Burnt and tortured earth.

The chapters of our shared history oppress me,
echoing and screeching through my core
like a madman yelling obscenities,
exhausting joy into a vacuous debt
that drives on and on.
Despair shuffles on the sidelines
covering like a dark dust cloak,
like a dried up well
going down and down
with no ending here.
No happy ending like Hollywood,
walking hand in hand into the sunset.

The sun is setting over our heart.
The clawed beast lumbers through scorched ground,
an ice crazed demon from hell, eating corpses from vast wars.
Scooping up heaps of bones from killing fields.
Pumping full its breast with dry blood and charred remains.
Holding up its prize of atomic arsenal,
crushing in that maddened claw
the turquoise jewel of Tibet.
Swirling black locusts chew through my brain.
The seal broken. The covenant split.
Pieces float in my mind.

2.

Edging past this frame in time,
I struggle to hold our prayer
and to turn the beads
that with each rotation
shape patterns of destiny.

In the wounded wasteland
where the fiery crucible
dries incessant waves
of sorrow and desire,
we sit and sweat away
our impurity in the fire.

A hushed prayer
rising phoenix like
heralding a resplendent potential,
the luminous pledge
already seated in our deathless mind.
This cool evening sunset.

3.

Yet this moment has its own hidden beauty, like a butterfly
fluttering on a summer's day in an English garden.
Delicate petals shimmer and long ago memories
of reclining in the sun, sinking into folds of sweet earth,
fingers moving sensuously through spring grass,
young and tender shoots.
Each detail interwoven and moving
outward from its innermost core
to resonate with the infinite order,
where we dream the nearest star
– so far away –

4.
I like to look up on a clear night,
my mind standing on tip-toe,
straining towards that dark void where stars blaze.
I long to be gathered up in flights of ascending spheres.

The birds are flying now, scattering any which way, maybe
Africa or the Great Lakes, who knows where. Ancestors
whisper in my night dreams. Ganesha drinks milk in London
temples. Sadhus scatter grey ash falling over the sceptics
heads, over their pin striped suits. Politicians stalk houses of
power as sacred pools of nectar dripping with maidens' milk,
soothe the fevered times of Shiva's return.

5.
With each turning page,
we revolve within eternal knots
unfolding a lone vastness
that arrives at the warmth of our touch.
Let our fingers touch lightly,
your skin, my skin.

Let our hearts creak open,
eroding hinges on the oak door,
of times beating,
wings moving in silence,
counting out the days.

I am moving towards my death
like a shy lover
moving towards the bridal chamber.
It is,
after all,
just another day.

Silent War Fields

In the twilight zone
desolate vague shapes
emerge slowly.
Retreating howls echo
in frenzied winds
blowing out life's desire.
Ice invades this wintry core –
already shredded.

Swallows above
moving to a new home
as we sleep in war fields
of blackened hearts
marching on a grey road
rolling into nowhere.
Springs of fresh life
cut
and falling
into freedom's mountain
of cold bodies.

Only a while ago singing voices
on a languid summer day,
chilled beer, coloured scarf,
laughter chiming the wind
painting a naïve view
as you kiss adieu.

Now trampling boots tear at roots
and life's longing lies forlorn
in a chilled pile.

Loss stares.
Death pierces.
No mercy
on a drunk crazed night
that knows no dawn.
Through blank eyes
humanity pours away
into deserts where sun scorches
and cacti grow.
Dry winds sweep
parched mouths
that taste
bitter prayers.

Angel of Death
working so silently
stitching the dead
into bundles of living
where the only movement
is to the earth below.
Skulls to dust
and dreams to the wind –
for another time.

For another age
that meets in the solace
only the patient earth can beg,
'Receive into your waiting womb
shattered spirits of the dead.'

In the dream of our remembrance,
covered by a field of silent crosses,
flowers appear.

The seal of our promise
from the cold, cruel grave,
buttercup and forget-me-not
germinate a new heralding
by night, by day,
I am seeking you
in the hope
that love
gently beholds
the place
where new life
softly
unfolds.

Legends

It is a time-consuming tale
that memory spins
through my empty dream,
while candle wax drips idly
onto my nearly full plate
as the grandfather clock, tick tocks.

A candle set at the altar
of my deserted birth
pleads that insistent penance,
needed once more for ancestral guilt.
In the darkened confessional box
beads of the rosary turn
at the corner of the weary road
where tinkers beg.
Sacred Heart and Mother Mary,
pray for us now and at the hallowed hour
and for all the time to come,
when knotted inside we spiral away
into lonely nights where courtesans prey.

Walking the wet avenue
on a cold winter's night
in severed cities built from strife.
Searching everyone's eyes
longing for connection,
only to see my separation.
The endless weeping,
broken promise and frail hope,
as I hold in aged hands
all that life can give,
then watch it slip away.

Here I petition,
with slow moving lips
in the chapel of our forgiveness,
the seed of my constancy.

'Lord I am not worthy to receive Thee
but only say the Word
and my soul will be healed.'
In the beginning was the Word.
In the beginning was already the end
and in the end the Word rested peacefully
in the field beyond all words.
Thy Kingdom is forever Come.

In the shrine on the hillside
where candles are lit for another time
from the beginning of time
to the last of time,
we pray for each other, earth and peace.

My candle flames low now,
and in that last flickering
life's longing
and cool prayers
mix with
frankincense and myrrh.

Recognition

The tides wash into a receding,
ocean vast, lone ship, tiny shell,
from the slow river wide.
Your faint echo
building to pressure
reaches my devotion.
Flames leap
into the black satin night.
Entering your icon
releases me
into the peaceful mandala
of our sure union.

A certain shimmer
of light on a sycamore leaf,
wild deer,
still presence,
memories of our meeting,
holding and stretching
to a startled silence.
My breath shallow
and heart pulsing
as I recognise the shared gaze.
Your light reflected in my soul.

The times I step away.

This Wound

Torn feeling,
solar plexus leaning
into heart pulsing
beating in rhythm,
marching on parade
to that far off place.

Fade that day
of my displaced gaze.

You are going away
into times ripping
through the still rose garden,
contained and locked
in this sealed pain.

A silent tear engulfs my world
as I walk on smiling,
spear in my heart,
under a night cloak.

Remainder

In that half-wasted night
dream shadows enter unbidden.
Memories
of love,
sweet cries softly moving
unlock blood and living water,
threaded colour under ice.
You, nourishing destroyer,
in your arrival
a farewell.

Cast out
to where the hungry howls
seep into my marrow.
In an instant,
it is clear.
You are not here.
Only a remnant of a dream.

Hope

1.
Howling the dark crazed sky,
thunder and hurricanes unleash
lightning flashing to earth.
Rain pours, washing away bridges
to chaotic descents.
Oceans rise, land erodes,
and certainty makes no sense.
Blind choices spin,
scheme and conspire.
Flames twist round thoughts
that contract and distract
in the heat of increasing solar fire.

2.
Yet, in that unguarded pause,
between this thought and the next,
hope awaits for the constant song
that angels murmur within our longing.
They breathe a shining
onto our uncertain pathways,
their voices lilting high
over fields of desolation.
Unformed words
speak of another time saying,
'We are the holders of your dream,
the whispering seed
planted in all cells,
the remainder of your journey
through the darkest of all times.'

3.
Thunder fades in distant hills
and rain soaks into ploughed fields.
In the still, still night of our return
frogs and crickets sing and wild lilies open.
Mists rise and stars emerge,
moonlight falls on silent faces
looking up from dreams faded.

Calling for hope
and angels appearing
in a world of images
that darkness veils.
While fear marches
earth writhes and ails
and greed prevails.

But when even hope vanishes
and things that can't be hoped for
disturb our waking night:
Then
in that ripe hour
distant bells summon
our hallowed ascension.
With jaws soft and hands open,
prayer turns to a new dimension.

4.
The movement beyond city voices.
A gentle wind that blows so quietly,
a silent singing from this turning earth,
a calm knowing of our life's worth.

Our timeless core unfolding,
the easy swing of the gate
opens
to glorify
a streaming purple light
confirming our communal sigh.

5.
As the veiled one comes before us,
the terror of separation
fades with an early bird call.
It is a dream only, of the fevered night.
The delicate smile of inner sight
reveals a knowing
within each breath
that keeps a holy world gathered
within spheres of our communion.

The deep sleep of remembering
awakens to dissolve our weaving through time.
Here we always are,
moving in the ancient stillness
with fluid steps
tracking a silent song
through the halls of our creation.
This timeless breath with you
my love.
It's been a long, cold, lonely night.

Your Call

I am looking long into this cool night
searching for a friend there.
But there is no one and nothing left to loosen.

My mask has fallen to the dust,
my tired arms gather the mountains
as my mind moving through space
fades without a trace.

The colours crimson and indigo
blaze bright across my wound of loss.
Though the finish never arrives,
my weary flesh offers its desire
and is fluid and soft.

Hidden icon of my heart,
seated serene
on your lion throne,
you know already
of my return.
Steps on your pathless way
invite my focus
beyond this mind's castle.
Yet still I wander
enchanted corridors,
forgetful and in pain.

Tonight, lying on your warm earth body
stars and planets shine their light.

Thumb and finger moving
slowly round your rosary,
as I feel our flowing breath
carry my yearning prayer.

In the pause between bead and breath,
longing and prayer,
I sense your sweet call.

Why not go naked?
It's better than the maze of the mind.

Openings

Unbinding

Move between the lines
to dissolve the tight myths
of unloved parts
that need careful kindness.

Unwrap the story lines
and passed down pain
put in place
with each buttoning
of your child's cloak.

Above all,
allow
the waterfall
of graceful belonging
within this universe,
(your true birthright),
to fill each cell
of your holy body.

New Day

This day has been dawning
a long time now
we've sat on warm stones
by the sacred fire
as the merry dance weaves on
through burial mounds
of long-ago years
where we lay ourselves down
in the sweet grasses of memory.

The flute that plays so cool
our time together.
So cool those days
on the scented pillow
where we shared love's secrets,
before the promise of awakening.

Fleeting familiar tunes
fast passing . . .
to where
now –
we let –
the silence –
in.

Time

Time has a way of equalising all things,
and what is important now will not be.
The ancient cities are piles of rubble,
even as the fashionable ones
shine like fireflies in the night.

The yearning to be powerful
betrays our lack of ease,
for in the kernel of the universe
there is profound peace.
Here choices are illusions
since there is nothing
from which we are apart.
The wanting,
already cooled,
as we no longer strive
but allow ourselves to arrive.

Transiting the halls of time,
aeons converge
into a constant returning
to where we can only be
lover and beloved
moving through eternity.

In the ruins of past empires,
our ancestors long gone,
our vanity whittled to the bone,
it is said,
'Time levels all things,
love, hate, day and night,
those taking birth,
those in the twilight.'

Marching on.
Time marches on
breathing flights of our desire
through the fire of longing,
consuming our many bodies,
in the days overtaking –
consuming me.

Time will balance all things
and what is wounded now
will be healed and set free.

Dharma Wheel

Full moon night,
planets glide through.
Thoughts circle away,
mind opens beyond
and drops
like an autumn leaf
meeting cool earth.

In this presence
no distance can measure.
No space can confine.
No time to know by.
The Buddha smiles
and holds a flower
for us to realise:

'All conditioned dharmas are
as dreams, illusions, bubbles, shadows,
like dew drops and a lightning flash.
Contemplate them Thus.'

Words echo on.
The Buddha spoke for forty years
and nothing was said.

Lord Buddha,
Just Dust Beneath Your Feet

I am
the heart of awareness
within this swirling universe,
a corridor of shadows and dreams
through which we pass.

I am a void;
all forms ebb and flow in me,
perpetually rising anew
from the cauldron of creation.

I am a cool fire consuming
that redeems all things
and bequeaths no trace.

Who am I?

I am a mystery,
the unknown knower
through whom space floats
and time spins.
My in breath forges all into a single whole.
Breathing out all forms
dissolve
within the axis mundi
to wonder
at the play of birth and death
while gazing softly
in still, equal view.

Hear the soundless turning as Gaia
transits the matrix of planets
within your vast body.
Lord Buddha,
Ganges and snow-capped Himalayas
absorbed in your grace,
the nectar of enlightenment
pouring from your eternal fount,
sustains all.
The roar of silence like a waterfall
flows through this infinite moment
in your abode.
It is blissful here – Knower of the Worlds.

Crossing this realm of duality
the deathless heart
relaxes apart
from the grid of karmic patterns
and the veil slips away.
Like a naked tree
dropping its leaves in trust of the new spring.
A restful beauty and the morning air nourishes
as awareness reverses the flowing stream
and the tempest transforms.

The city of skulls
turns to dust.
And blowing amidst the ash,
that Ark,
that still point
which carries all potential . . .

Like this morning, I bow.

Lord Buddha,
my head has touched the dust
beneath your peaceful lotus feet.

Walk Your Way

The Buddha stands fearless,
not wobbling like my unsure legs
that try to support
the glory of his ascending spiral
which meets the expanding horizon
where peace rests amid chaos.

No fear, no suffering, no delusion.
Walk your journey calmly upon this earth,
the graceful trees shelter and
the dusk moon is rising to sanctify your way.

The Other Shore

While skylarks sing
black ravens alight easily
on the green sycamore tree.
With casual eye they look
at children shaping mansions of fantasy.
A raven lifts its wings effortlessly
gliding over distant fields as children run to tea.

Since I do not aspire to return again,
warm kissed lips
have turned to cool quiet prayers.
Savouring senses thirst
in the field of desire
swooping to secure
in the slippery mire
all that turns
to a smouldering funeral pyre.
The swing is empty now,
moving to and fro in the country park.

Children play out fantasies
while lovers stroll among summer roses
and magnolia trees.
Shadows fall across the veranda
on an evening sunset;
satisfied murmurings and chinking glasses
wrap all in that sleepy feeling
as we drift and forget.

Yet, the Buddha raised his sword to say:
'Grasping birth leads to decay.'

All the words I've learnt to say
are slipping from my brain
into this house of fire.
The children play in a cemetery,
the raven gliding to its tree.
Bewildering appearances come like dreams
as death erodes my solidity.
Lotus and moon seat
dwelling above the heat,
in the essence of awareness
rests all that troubles us no more.

When the wind blows gently and the long grass
bends to its caress,
when apples, pears and peaches hang abundant on the trees
and birds feather their nests.
When children play with coloured stones
and mothers cook the daily fare,
warm bread rises and rivers run to the sea.
When I look with love at this turning tide
and feel the arrow paining deeply,
I hear the whisperings of the world to come
and all that is forever ceasing.

Let the angels smile,
let them laud all of creation,
the children and the raven.
Let us taste and exalt
the sweet and the salt,
and so the winds will whisper
and the sun has shone
on those already
'Thus Gone'.

Tathagata

Come in from the storm,
there is no rain here.
The floods that wash from birth to death,
have dried,
and the winds that shape our destiny,
are still.

Come in and release from your holding.
Let your enchanted house dissolve;
it has no use any more.
With one in-breath
feel the further reaches of your being
gather the entire cosmos.
Breathe out and let your still joy
suffuse the atoms.

All things always are,
the rise and fall,
when time is no more.

I Dream of You HH

Last night I dreamt of you Dalai Lama,
your kind smile and gracious bow.
So deep your river runs
in our wish to merge
with Amitabha light of wisdom.
You unravel and fill the emptiness,
gathering a million Ganges' sand grains.
Yet appearance is still here within lucid dream
lacking in substance.
What is it?

This moment in life,
all sentient beings
are suffering.
It is real enough.
Who do we save?
And
What is it?

Mind Like Sky

Let us slip away
and wander softly
along the banks of the midnight river.
Damp grass between our toes,
sweet jasmine in the air.
Let us walk from the glowing coals
and traverse all views at this time.

What are these spinning day dreams
tangled in roots of thought
entwining a depth of need
in a thicket of craving,
exhausting my endless bodies.
Like fire flaming through a night forest.

This talk of enlightenment,
what is it and where do we go?
Renunciation and shaven head,
working my fingers round the mala
in the night and to the dead,
as I long for release
into your veiled core.

Vajra Guru.
Diamond jewelled.
Intricate patterns are embroidered
in the heart ground you rule.
Primordial mind like the sky,
my spirit and my form
you illumine and edify.

You gather in the rose and the thorn;
like rain drops to the river,
you take my body when it is worn.

Each day of my mindful practice
among the ruins
I walk to and fro,
holding at my chest,
the gift
of your rare cameo.

Christ – the Rose Apple Tree

1.
I am the vast fields
ploughed into furrows
stretching to the machine,
black ravens and white seagulls
coast behind tyres turning,
turning into the land.
The tips of ripe wheat
drift into sunflowers
and green English lawns
where tea and scones wait
unattended at the polite hour.

The sun is opening me
as far as I can go.
Christ the rose apple tree
breathes stillness in the garden
where African swallows gather.

2.
You are the stone
upon which we are shattered.
Dreams float in sunbeams,
bleached pyramids in deserts
stretching to Northern landscapes.
In half light, silhouetted children
run slowly into the infinite;
their muffled joy evaporates
into silent skies.
It is empty.
The landscape is empty
as slowly we spin through life's desire.

3.
You are the great fields
and I have come to plant my seeds.
Floating somewhere in the storm,
I bow down to you
as a moth to a flame
meets its certain fate.
Inferno dust adorns the way
as we wander into an unknown day.
Weavers of the web enfold,
the seeds of our constancy
echo in our dreams at night.

Wild geese ready to migrate
as the wheel turns to where
the promise we await
flows through our veins
confirming our hallowed estate.
Here revealed
is the emerging light.
Weavers of the web
wake from your long dream tonight;
show your face to the dawn unicorn.
Bliss is the flowering of this way.

4.
With hands open and grace descending,
the painful journey of love
winds through our veins.
Praise to that strange descent
and stranger still to arrive
where hearts entwine
and where it's not clear
what is yours and what is mine.
Nous avons été remplis de ta vie,
qui n'aura pas de fin.

We have been filled with your life
which has no end.
You, who laid the foundation,
whose compassion opened the skies,
who was left here to die.

Christ, the rose apple tree,
as you sustain your promise
bells ring through the delicate night.
When we wake from our long sleep,
we can wonder again and again
at your brief appearing.

Fornalutx – Furnace of Light

Nada te turbe – nada te espante,
quien Dios tiene nada le falta.
Nada te turbe, nada te espante.
Solo Dios basta.

Fornalutx, Furnace of Light,
your darshan opens a sacred space
when the pull to another
invites vulnerability.
Nada te turbe . . . let nothing trouble you,
Nada te falta . . . with God – you will not shatter.
Solo Dios basta – God alone is enough.

Furnace of Light,
your darshan ripples out
and healed for a moment
I fracture with the next wave.
The seed and egg broken
in the fields where hunters intersect
with death and peril,
chance and skill.

Suffering is separation
and the many faces of Your eventual joy.
You knock on my door
in the sound of wind circling
the lonely hillside monastery,
in the shutters banging and a dog howling,
in the village festivity below.

Nada te espante . . .
let nothing frighten you.
You enter my core
in the laughter of friends,
in the hot sun warming my skin,
in taking bread and café,
in slipping into the warm sea.
Quien a Dios tiene nada le falta . . .
Whoever has God lacks nothing.

Beyond the guarded gate
gathered into that source
of our beginning and end,
You dwell constant
softening strategies
that hold against a forgotten land.
The light – as fear burns to dust:
The rising radiance
wakes from borrowed dreams
that diminish the glory
of our resting now and forever.
And for all the days to come
in the unknowing heart space,
the constant stream
into which we all fall.
Faith will carry us across.

Nada te turbe,
let nothing trouble you,
let the dawn sun enter your closed door.
Weave the waves of your sacred life,
the dark and the light,
into a magnificent cloak
that shelters from the storm.

The evening storm sweeping past
and the smell of fresh cut grass,
the candle flame flickering
in the coloured night glass.
This day only,
only ever this day,
this moment
beyond the crying times,
beyond all the times
to the ripened time
that will carry us across.

I am trusting –
trusting this presence,
this unknowing,
the river that carries us through.
Trusting You.

Nada te turbe, nada te espante,
Quien Dios tiene, nada le falta.
Nada te turbe, nada te espante
Solo Dios basta.
God alone is enough.

Sadhu

Tight and safe
social faces
seeking approval
in the market place,
where we traded desires.

Restless,
pacing lost cities that echo
a lack of holy presence.
It's a wasteland
through which we dream
the ancient path
that myths and lore have told,
crossed by awakened ones of old.

A glimpse only
and the ocean of tears cried,
with illusions snare
now broken, dried.
Longing songs heard,
the last days of the tide
turning from the tribe,
who can say why?

Touch of the divine,
opening into shadowed crossings
where questions have no answers,
where waiting on the emptiness
we bow again and again
to live this laughing,
crying,
suffering and dying.

Being born again
like whores for your grace.
Others say it is madness,
let them say what they like.

No writing, no temple can satisfy this wandering.
We are the ones in search of you:
who is before and after all existence,
who stands patient until the end of time,
who merges fire and water in a joyful breath,
who is and is not,
the nearest of all friends.
Who, beyond time and space,
spins the daily tale,
who meets us at the gateway
and beyond all crossings.

Most subtle of beings,
our very essence:
empty and full,
everywhere and nowhere,
path and fruit,
that which prompts us to wander.
From your vast store house
yield your numerous blessings.

Our feet are covered with ashes.

Pathfinder –
light our way home.

Shiva's Footprint

Turning chaos and breathing cosmos
dissolving earth in tidal waves and volcano.
Battlefield of dancers moving in slow motion,
while speeding up, speeding up.
Blue moon disc,
colour, sitar, lights and festival
fill the festering street.
People shoving
as screams and cries fade into night.
Night on a boat with silver moon sliver
floating carefree down the Ganges.
Still and vast.

Perpetual hunger for life,
you drive on.
Red passion and energy reaching to the throat,
sighing in ecstasy,
then in sorrow for love lost
into the hardness of a vain mask.
Your whirl of emotion
moves
to the drum
– beating time –
running out.
Water
through grasping hands.

In serene Samadhi
rapt within the heart cave,
your deathless eye observes
seed and egg spinning toward each other
in love or lust.

The drum beat turning
dispassionately
to cracking of skulls at Varanasi.

Fire dust and ashes fall into the slow river
floating carefree towards night.
Consciousness expands blending with light,
love and weeping tears slide
into chaos turning to order.
All within the dancer's footprints
dancing this life,
this world,
this shimmering creation.

Nataraja,
Lord of the Dance,
dancing the heart of each one.
Tell us, what is freedom?

Why worry, why strive?
For I am arrived.
I am Shiva.

What do I care for life or death,
for illusion or enlightenment?
I am constant,
I dwell in my own heart,
I am Shiva
in whom nothing is
and nothing is not.

I say:
This universe turns
just for the love of it.

The Garland

The river flows so freely
through the conch shell sounding
on this new day dawning
washing past the sandbanks
of these many lives counting.
The times unfold
circles of our prayers
that echo the searing call,
silent and wordless.

Beyond the dust of everyday roaming
through the streets of our distraction,
I place
in the early morning
a marigold and daisy garland
to adorn your footprint
in the cavern of my heart.

Nothing and Everything

The embrace of cool peace
that enters past
my layered ochre robe
where Yes
is the freedom
to connect
with a graceful breath
that allows all things
into the releasing heart
which needs
Nothing.

because

From within
this flesh body
spiralling energy spheres
ripple through
all forms
resonating
with the silent hymn
sung by gospel singers
proclaiming that
the winding stairs
lead to the one
that knows itself as
Everything.

The Return

The Return

Behind crimson curtains
with gypsy netting in shadows
crocheted so fine,
the Lady of Avalon waits her time.
Outside that dark edge of night
washes over again
as we wrap away our layered selves
and silent wounds,
long slipped into the night secret.
As morning arrives
into just the way
we breathe black space and stars
before the half rose and yellow light,
sunrise and birdsong.

Across the dawning fields
half formed in misty oak vales,
warrior soldiers move
across the centuries
in tune with the patriarch's step.
They advance slowly
to where the white goddess remains
– these long cycles –
toppling heads of lofty abstraction
to sever this cold command.

Her tuneful violin dreams
joyous notes soaring and warm blood,
bringing songs to our voices.

The music flows to the land of awakening
and whispers within tides turning,
softening the very centre of our chest.

Here is the voice once dreamed of
emerging from the jewelled locket
hidden in silence,
seated within each turn of the rosary,
encoded in the mystery
and drifting on mighty seas.

Here is the deep promise
of this longed for
wedding night.

The River Flows Through

The river flows through
as I am woven
together with you.
Like threads in a blanket
that keeps us warm
beyond the tide
of that which
does not recognise
the gentle devotion
of us together.
This still presence
nurtures and soothes
my quiet woe,
like a song
with notes entwining,
like lovers
secure in their chateau.

Lady of the Night,
you come to me
in the people
through whom
I move.

'What I offer'
you say,
'Is what you have already.'

Goddess of the Night

Slow death of the honeyed maiden
made acceptable by acquiescence
of her power bleeding
into the growing machinery
which rolls on,
smashing its blind way
through petalled valleys
of cornflower blue,
swaying gently
in the midnight
sweet grass breeze.

Ruler of the Night,
reach into our pain
after the red glow
of the setting sun
when moon haze shrouds
fields of ancient chestnut trees.

Your truth
like standing stones
rises from the earth in great stillness.
Your power
like a phoenix
blazes from ashes of smouldering fury.
Sweeping across the doorstep
into my hidden place
your compassion,
Dark Lady,
emerges on the other side
of clear Buddha light.

Your depth,
Queen of Thunder,
creates fearless energy
which flows in my veins
mixing intoxicated oxygen with blood,
pouring forth ecstatic and chaotic
flowing from my mouth and hands outstretched
into grief transformed,
as you roar through the lands
your healing
sacred earth sounds.

Flying the Night

Yell out
beyond whispered corsets
and thin stick catwalk.
Nice girls
enshrined
virgin mary
smashed and shattered
flames round burning witch
radiate bright her power
of Kali unleashed.

Your thunderous steps
through wind and fire
dance the seasons' choir.
We want
to mingle in your essence
to never be caught
to smash domestic chaining
to fly together in the winged night time
to drink from the skull
your fearless energy sublime.

Owls and foxes appear
at the dawn of ordered tomorrows.
No wonder you shake,
centuries' suppression
before
Mother Shakti's stare.

Burning Ghat

It is a long time
since I've heard the birds
after a night like this.
Embers of the fire
reflecting times burnt down.
House half constructed,
already passed
into the matrix of her energy body.

Dark Snake Queen
your presence announces
with sudden chill,
your latest kill.
Is it a mistake or a lie,
do we laugh or do we cry
as you reap your vast harvest
with barely a sigh.

Lady of Desire's End,
with random swoop
you come from behind,
you come from the side.
In the shadows you move;
weaving patterns of ruin
you fulfil karma's law
with a simple yawn
of your terrible jaw.
Devouring old and young alike,
even babies you strike.

Devourer of the Many Worlds,
your mouth a cavern of eternity
into which we all fall
while offering a fervent entreaty.
Drenched in blood
you display your skull necklace.
You mount a pile of bones
as you flaunt your fearful dress.

Ruler of Time,
in wars, a holocaust or worse,
famine or some other curse
gathering a million, maybe more
eating last breaths and failing thoughts,
reducing a life to naught.
Looking straight into the immensity
you whisper your austere finality,
'all of you will be touched by me.'

Initiator through Suffering,
when I feel your intimate gaze
I pray my soul
with dread no trace,
'Come, my amazing Kali,
resplendent and mighty,
I wait the long days
for our destined embrace.'

Life – Uncertain

I am open to you,
my shield put aside,
fears to the wind.

The journey begins
with a risk.
Uncertain is our way.
Long is the day.

This faith,
at first a waterfall,
then deep and lyrical
through the heart land
so mythical
on and on
it goes
through your icon
so slow
trusting that soon,
back into you,
this journey flows.

Queen of Heaven,
Lady threading day stars
with pearls, mantras and azaleas,
your subtle hint
softens resistance
and makes me live
beyond the realm of death.

Black Madonna

Your love
moves as music
in the valley
opening to
a sweet and tender place
where rhythms dance
a melting vigilance.

It plucks the deep
strings of my soul
sounding notes
into every level
divine and human,
and all union
we attempt
in shy and clumsy ways.

That sound carries
across the vast
fields of lifetimes
yielding into
the mystery
that you are.

Kuan Yin Across the Fields

At the end of a perfect day
across flat and cold winter fields,
naked trees bow and sway
in an endless wind
that blows
my thoughts away.

As I lay
huddled under warm blankets,
the breath of my loved one
listeth and wills into the
dark night's embrace.
Moonlight peeps under curtains
which billow and chase
an unseen wind that howls and moans
through cracks in the window frame.

Warm breath and cool wind
carry to a distant bell
that chinks and chimes
recklessly in time
with the bark of a lone dog.
A gate against its post
knocks strange memories
safe to ponder in my night cocoon,
my night time womb.

Dream steps to Kuan Yin's light
where gently, imperceptibly
our spirits roll and skip
in silent secret ecstasy.

In the black black night
of your return
a spark of joy
at the inevitability
of our promised unity.

Across the fields
I hear your vow,
'All beings are nestled in me,
all time,
all possibility,'
as the wind listeth where it will,
until . . .
until . . .

Mother of the Buddhas

I am floating,
buoyant and unfolding
within your cosmic womb,
subtle dawn of creation,
Mother of the Buddhas,
initiator and feeder of my needs.
I am content feeling your perpetual keep,
your warm juice and sweet nectar nourish me.
Your deep waves of breath
open and empty my lungs,
like night and day,
the aeons appear as dust
in your single eye.

Kuan Yin who rides a dragon,
who plants the seed
over many lifetimes
of the unbroken vow,
I breathe in you, swim in you,
soften and thaw into you.

I hear muffled symphonies
howls and whisperings
in the halls of time,
pausing before the door
to be born again
into this house of fire.
We'll meet at the forgetting home
where suffering burns deep into bone.

As we wander on,
the Buddha said,
'Leave this home,

move on like a swan
or as a bee tasting honey only.
Be free to roam
but see all as a dream,
like bubbles,
like foam.'

Ma, you say,
'Stay and Be.
To the cries of this world,
listen carefully.'

Ma, you mingle with me
as the scent of a summer rose in the breeze.
As a distant memory haunting
or a shadow I can never catch or hardly see.
As a pain at the core which never heals
and does not cease.

Ma, I am your refugee,
but why should I flee.
In the dark hushed night
celestial bodies expand
and contract before me.
They praise your glory Ma,
Crazy Ma
Sweet Ma
Wild Ma
Om Ma
Floating Free Ma
Walk Away with the Victory Ma.

Celebration

Unknowing

If you wish to enter the door
through which the sages go,
then bow your head to the floor
and rise again more deeply
into that –
which thoughts cannot know.

If you wish to tread the pathless path,
dive into the well of cool fire
where mystics silently grow.

Floating Worlds

The inner dissolving
of armoured walls
that traces so lightly
the expanding possibilities
of our high and low notes.
Together in that lightness
towards the end of creation,
we harvest floating particles
throughout the cosmos.

This attraction to another
in the kernel of the universe
where all life starts,
a warm kiss opens beyond
where death can go.

The mythic dance yearns
in the desert of night
as stormy shadows move over
a wild bloom flowering,
the perfume so sweet
of this reverie together.

So quietly beads turn.
Tender words of the mystic,
floating in my ear.

The Bay

Wild geese calling,
thousands flock to the sea
swooping over the bay
stretching before my eyes,
a brush-stroke
of blue and grey.

Water meets sky,
waves meet clouds.
Seals frolic and
a still Gaelic song rises
infusing the spirit of Ireland.
The mind is space,
full
of beginnings and ends
knitted into a Celtic knot.

Geese land,
blissful and silent,
cold and bleak,
sky, mind and sea.

Waves on the Water

Waves on the water
ripple through my mind.
A distant sound
of the night train
carries my dream
over the threshold
where a hushed ease
stops all time.

Within the pause
past and future
rhythms
of the insistent lure
merge
within the sound
and the waves
float
ten thousand worlds
dissolving
to reveal limitless mind
balanced
in the opening of a rose petal,
in the oceans lapping at the shore.
In the Heart Sutra
rippling out from every being's core.

Between crest and fall,
flowing in and flowing out
I wake this dawn
to a faraway call.

The Only Way

Conception rises from the land,
fire descends from light.
Feel the flow of the universe
coursing through your veins.
Feel the leap in your heart as death approaches.
Laugh all day at the inane,
cry all night for the pain.
Lay your head down
and gently say,
love is the only way.

Sunbird

I am a caged bird
tied to illusions
of safe and secure times.
My wings beat against
fear's arrival
in the structures we build
against the shifting tide.

In the waking of dedication
my feathers unfold
while venturing to another land.
In my longing courage grows,
to let gold adornments fall
in the back-streets
of my shadowed past,
to fly the thermal stream
that lifts away from this vain play.

There I'll soar free
from times gone
where the midnight muse
with each turn of the tulsi bead
writes words of our completion.

Homage to you – Himalaya

Holy and Blessed Himalayas,
from the great earth you rise,
ethereal and immutable.

In your lap dwells the eternal Shiva,
through your peaks roams the breath of Ram.
From your heart flows the sacred Ganga
bringing faith to humanity below.

Holy mountains,
transcendent and inaccessible,
you absorb the worlds sounds
that ever circle
your infinite and silent vigilance.

Your timelessness saturates my world.
Thoughts cannot capture your elusive mystery,
your divine dignity,
your transparent ecstasy.

How lovely to gaze and wonder.
How could I forget,
how could I doubt
your endless grace?

Sub Ek – All One

This stuff of my body
arises from the same source
as earth, sky and tree.
This mind
momentarily arising
is woven from so many threads
into an endless tapestry.
Altogether there is nothing separate
from this source within which all exists.

That source cannot be named.
Only let the fire of suffering
burn away resistance
to the transformation
initiated by the inner call
which seeks only
to return
all.

Emerald Crystal

Let us wait upon the hour
the night of our dreams,
the earth will sing
and we will bind
the severed ends
of our sacred ring.

Let us wait upon the hour
where hearts unfold
mixing turquoise and gold,
where water falls
in tropical forests
and the lush song
lifts waves at sea
that carry us to a perfect shore.

Let us dream the hour
that threads our folk lore.
Our luminous essence
will shine a light,
so from core to skin
our jewelled earth
will radiate the bright.
And we will

Stop –

and consider,
the wild flowers,
the humming bird,
the moon and stars,
the emerald crystal.

Avalon

As we go on less is familiar,
for in age pretensions fall away.
Standing plump with breasts drooping,
wrinkled at the brow
while a rapid world
pushes past our poignant memories.

Our life passes soon
like butterflies rising from a cocoon.
All too quickly wings are faded,
though sweet to taste this moment –
sweet to taste your gaze
turned towards me.

Ah, the mellow winds blow so lightly
while past karmas burn away.
As we stand simple in the core
of our remembrance,
there are no secrets anymore.
The planes are flying overhead
but let them go and continue walking,
hand in hand,
round the edges of our life.

In Avalon, in another age,
we'll be holding hands across lifetimes.
I'll await you there at the Chalice Well;
my sweet one, our hour is passing.
I'll meet you there
to share the bloodied crystal cup,
and again
we'll walk the night alone.

Silently Age Dawns

As the great wheel of time
rolls silent
through this intimate
transcendent heart,
like beads of the rosary
round and round.

So now,
the years dissolve
as wrinkles grow,
the last pieces of embroidery thread
already placed
into our intricate icon.
Our hearts trembling
as we near the Beloved
and bow our head.
Finished for now,
our lives gently hanging
by a shred.

Maybe,
we can smile
a little more
at the stories of our life.

Simple Sense of Being

Here we all are,
breathing and dreaming
as brown ducks quack
and herons fly with outstretched necks
while turtles paddle around
enjoying their simple sense of being.

While subtle is the path of heart
which unfolds the expanding present
to reveal an inner point of the timeless void,
within which all appears and disappears
in a magical dance that moves to a silent tune
and leads to bowing at the lotus feet,
where we learn that love is the greatest gift.

And it is grace to know
that suffering can turn to joy
and joy is the place where all belongs.
And joy turns to peace
as the ancient way of the heart
whispers at sunrise and sunset.
In the pauses between certainty
when the known track evaporates,
rain pours onto parched land
in the promise
that all things interconnect.

And faith has its own beauty
when eyes are too dim to see,
when we forget our worries
and allow ourselves just to be.

While here we all are,
breathing and dreaming,
dreaming and breathing
as brown ducks quack, herons fly
and turtles paddle around.
And
subtle is the path of heart.

Fire Minder

At the end of a long day,
as dusk falls,
embers in the fire cool.
She turns and walks away.
What was all the fuss about?
Who knows . . .
No more time to think and worry.
Only stillness remains.
Silence settles
and the fire minder is no longer seen
as she merges into night.

This poem is dedicated to Seekers and Lovers of the Dharma. With gratitude in particular to my Noble Teachers and friends from the Forest Sangha who have provided much spiritual nourishment, guidance, inspiration and 'grist for the mill'.

Closing poem . . .

Offering

Do not worry about tomorrow
for see how this day unfolded
without the need of fear.
Look again at all that supports you –
breath, sun, friend and aspiration –
and offer your life instead
in formless quiet prayer.

Closing homage . . .

The time came for Ram to die and so he asked the whereabouts of Hanuman . . .

Hanuman came bounding down from the sky. He hit the ground with a thud like a thunderstone. He was right close to Rama, smiling at him, laughing and happy.

'Oh Hanuman!'

'My King!' Hanuman knelt before Rama.

Rama said, 'As long as men shall speak of you, you will live on Earth. No one can equal you. Your heart is true; your arms are strong; you have the energy to do anything. You have served me faithfully and done things for me that couldn't be done.'

'It's nothing,' said Hanuman, 'I am your friend, that's all.'

Rama wore a rare golden bracelet set with gemstones on his right arm, a costly irreplaceable ornament inherited from among the wealth of the Solar Kings from ancient days. He said, 'Best of monkeys, take this as my gift,' and gave it to Hanuman.

Hanuman snatched the bracelet from Rama and started to turn it over and around in his white furry paws, looking closely at it. Then he bent and broke it, he twisted the gold and pulled out the jewels, and put them between his hard teeth. He bit down on the priceless gems and broke them like nuts, and carefully searched over the pieces, looking everywhere for something.

Rama asked him, 'Monkey at a time like this why are you still difficult?'

Hanuman answered, 'Lord, though this bracelet looked expensive it was really worthless, for nowhere on it did it bear your name. I have no need of it Rama. What do I want with anything plain?'

Vibhishana sniffed at that. 'Then I can't see what value life has to you Why don't you destroy your body as well?'

Then with his sharp fingernails Hanuman tore open his breast and pulled back the flesh. And see! There was written again and again on every bone, in fine little letters – Rama, Rama, Rama, Rama, Rama . . .

Rama – with his two hands pressed together Hanuman's parted flesh, and the wound over his beating heart came together leaving no scar at all, not even one big as a grain of dust, on the tip of a hair. Rama drew off his hand his broad gleaming gold ring that said 'Rama', the ring that Hanuman carried to Sita. He put it onto Hanuman's wet bloodstained paw and gently closed his monkey fingers over it.

Who is this monkey Hanuman? Rama has let him loose in the world. He knows Rama and Rama knows him. Hanuman can break in or break out of anywhere. He cannot be stopped, like the free wind in flight.

Hanuman can spot a tyrant, disguises and words of talk cannot confuse a mere wild animal. Hanuman's rescue of brave poets in any peril may be had for their asking, and that monkey will break the handsome masks of evil kings.

Hanuman will take your sad tune and use it to make a happy dance. We have seen that white monkey. Strong is his guard. Especially take warning, never harm a free poet.

The Son of the Wind. The warm, dry night wind, and all the trees swaying! I don't care for love or death or loneliness – here comes the high Wind, and what am I . . . ?

With appreciation and gratitude for:

My mother, father and brothers who came first, my sweet grandma and my strong grandma who came before first. Janie and Moe Weinberg for love, generosity and support. Maharaji Neem Karoli Baba, Guru of Gurus. Ajahn Chah who said to me, 'Look to your own heart.' Master Hua for opening the Kuan Yin Dharmas. H.H. Dalai Lama for Bodhisattva vows. Ajahn Sumedho for blazing the trail and making the Path seem possible. John Coleman for bravely teaching the first ten day retreats in England. Mrs U Myat Saw, my first Buddhist mother, Noy Thomson, my second. Those who inspire walking the way, particularly Ram Dass for sharing so very much. Ajahn Sucitto, Ajahn Munindo and Heng Sure for their complete dedication to the way. Anando for opening the door. Candasiri, Sundara and Rocana for their enormous courage and strength. Martine Batchelor for first shaving my head. Abhassara and Medhanandi for poetry and music. Vimala, Cintamani, Siripanna, Satima for special friendship. All the Sisters, past, present and future. Barbara Jackson for my first poetry book, Pamela Nada and Ges for my first empty writing book. Cathy Wickham for keeping the faith, Joanne Fedler for warmth, Katrin for laughter and understanding. Sylvia and Judy for our work together. Ian and Maxine for 'being with how it is now'. Maura and Franklin Sills for the gift of Karuna. All those who entered, left and stayed in the monastery. Angel for keeping the bread coming, Beata O'Donoghue for keeping our bodies going. Father Paul and Father John for blessing my marriage. Satish for blessing this book. Kelvin Williams for making our move to South Africa possible. Chrisi and Louis for so much in South Africa. Brid and Liam, Andrea and Dermod for warm hospitality. Narayano and Jitindriya for appreciating the lila. Douglas and Magaret Jones, Grazia, Greta, Sarah Miles, Elizabeth West, Oriana, Becky, Junaq, Anne, Pat and Alta. Sioux and Alan. Bamboo mountain and the Umzimkulu River. My nephew Daniel Peacock and niece Elisha Peacock. All those that have supported our work. Last and not least, Jack.

To the Beloved in all your many guises.

Thanissara (Mary Peacock) was born in 1956 into a Catholic Irish/ Anglo family in London and later entered Art School in Southampton. In 1975 she encountered Buddhist practice and teachings which led her to travel to India and the East staying in ashrams and monasteries. After meeting the meditation master Ajahn Chah in Thailand at the age of 22 she was inspired to ordain as a Buddhist nun. She lived in that discipline for 12 years being involved in the beginnings of the Western Theravadin nuns order in the UK.

In 1991 she left the order and married. Together with her husband, Kittisaro, she leads Buddhist meditation and inter-faith retreats in many different countries. In 1994 they moved to South Africa and are presently guiding teachers of the Buddhist Retreat Centre, Ixopo, and have established a small hermitage, Dharmagiri, in the Drakensberg Mountains. In response to both the AIDS crisis and poverty in their local area, they have established an Outreach Programme which mainly focuses on supporting nearby rural schools and the training of Home Based Care workers to support health and well-being in the local community.

Thanissara's work is totally dependent on donations and the principle of sharing. One of her concerns is that as the Buddhist culture interacts with the more economically empowered 'Western' societies, it maintains an awareness of the greater global discrepancies between wealth and poverty, North and South. It is her hope that this awareness will encourage a wise and compassionate engagement that extends beyond sectarianism and beyond the walls of meditation centres and monasteries.